LEGENDS OF THE SPOTLIGHT

LEGENDS OF THE SPOTLIGHT

FELIX NORTHWOOD

CONTENTS

1 Introduction to the World of Icons and Celebrities — 1

2 Historical Perspectives on Fame and Celebrity — 3

3 The Evolution of Celebrity Culture — 5

4 Iconic Figures in Film and Television — 9

5 Musical Legends: From Rock 'n' Roll to Hip-Hop — 11

6 Fashion Icons and Style Influencers — 15

7 Sports Heroes and Athletic Icons — 19

8 Political Icons and World Leaders — 23

9 The Dark Side of Fame: Scandals and Tragedies — 25

10 Behind the Scenes: Untold Stories and Anecdotes — 27

11 Legacy and Impact: Icons in Popular Culture — 31

12 Conclusion: Reflections on the Power of Celebrity — 35

Introduction to the World of Icons and Celebrities

As a famous person, sometimes you would have always felt alone and certainly are not by chance that many of them often find themselves living alone and with addictions that torment them. Always remaining in the footsteps of the great star, we will take some beautiful ideas from their sometimes incredible stories, and we will understand what you do not have to do in a famous person... in order not to have your story included in any other book that one day talks about the fall! This chapter journeys with you through the chapters of our book where we take a look at some celebrated singers and musicians, TV and movie personalities, athletes, models, writers, and political and religious leaders. Some very sad stories and some not-so-memorable tales.

An icon can only be an icon if it has a story. This book is full of stories that reveal aspects of some of the world's most beloved icons. All have very different, very human stories – some beautiful, some ugly, some amazing, and some depressing. We hope that the range of different experiences of fame and influence of these 50 people will engage you, make you think and keep you wondering about what draws us all to the 'stars'. They are people who have often been in the spotlight and usually have influenced millions of people. And many believed that as famous people they had something different in their hearts.

Defining Icons and Celebrities

Icons and celebrities are easily recognized, but often difficult to define concretely due to the inherently vague nature of these terms. The most common definition of celebrity is "a famous person," and many would refer to an icon simply as a "very famous person." However, this idea of "fame" does not reveal the distinctions of why some are seen as icons while others are simply admired. Indeed, scholars disagree on what the distinctions should actually be between the two terms. Regardless of academic definitions, generally society has come to recognize two primary criteria that define an individual as either an icon or a celebrity: presence and impact.

Both icons and celebrities have a level of presence and impact in their area of expertise, but icons have presence and impact at both a cultural level and a personal one. No children will grow up having never heard of Picasso or Beethoven, no adult will go long without hearing their works lauded in public, and many in almost every home will have some idea of who they are if they present an image of their face or play a single bar of their music. "Celebrity" is often derided for its shallowness and its reliance on TMZ and reality shows, but "icon" brings to mind an entirely different kind of person. True icons carry within their stories not only the memories of what made them great, but also the communities that uplifted them—be they a community of basketball fans, jazz enthusiasts, or any other demographic. To be iconic is, in other words, to tell a piece of not only a personal story but also a cultural one.

CHAPTER 2

Historical Perspectives on Fame and Celebrity

Fame and stardom are not modern inventions. The notion of the "famous" ever reverberates in the literature and arts of earlier periods of history. In ancient Greece, the traditional bards, such as the Muses and Clio, each inspire those whom they favor to cultivate a good reputation or famous name wider than life. Homeric heroes are epically noted with epithets such as "swift-footed Achilles," expanding on their attributes and accomplishments. The narratives about Plato and Socrates introduce an academic notation of fame or ignominy, even among relative strangers. Harriet Mayor Fulford admits that, "celebrity is not new. First-century Greeks and Romans were eager as we are to watch a reality show."

Roman funerary stones articulate that athletes, especially charioteers, actors, poets, politicians, and combats of gladiatorials and men were popular in the fame of the social setting. Approximately three hundred funeral epitaphs signify enactment stars drawn on stage in shows of exotic wild animals. Those deaths in the amphitheater areas near the Circus Maximus emphasized their feats as gladiators. Many African performers who died in or near Rome as actors or gladiators were the leading celebrities here. Such a conflation of stage stardom and societal privilege invites research on how familiar the stardom status acknowledgments are in comparative anthropologies of performance, spectacle, and society. Many of the earliest Roman actors were drawn from the lowest ranks of slave-importance.

Ancient Notions of Fame and Celebrity

People have been discussing fame and stardom for as long as there have been people. "One learns, just as one has learned in Vienna, where heads turn towards the Einsteins and the Freuds of the street, that there are spots in America where the native mows his lawn on Saturdays some yards from the garage of the famous," writer Philip Wylie marveled in 1949 in the proto-tabloid essay collection Generation of Vipers. In this, Wylie's observations are attained through—and are conditioned by—the muscle of an intellectual paradigm a professional scholar will not be able to avoid running into. Curiously, though this ancient fascination goes at some point unaccounted for by Eliade, our understanding of the past is not ill-served by his framework.

The blind singer Demodocus, also reportedly from Chios, figured into more than a few stories we have and seems to have been a frequent topic of discussion on his own account. According to Plutarch, he was so popular in Rome that people acknowledged and admired him on the streets of the capital. So was Antandros too small to believe, or did he leave behind a legitimately world-class "name for himself"? Indeed, it's curious to think about how a name or fame of Demodocus's scale can be the result of only one tale's worth, never mind spinning further stories. And yet, just as Achilles is forever worth hearing about, so is Demodocus. He has not captivated readers from so many centuries removed on the strength of a song or two, nor has our interest in him been driven by tradition unmeditated upon.

CHAPTER 3

The Evolution of Celebrity Culture

Celebrity culture is an ever-evolving complex, born out of many different intricacies that mark the zeitgeist of that era. Classical Hollywood celebrities, adored by mass audiences, whilst iconic in their own right, have since changed into celebrities that attract niche audiences. Now, celebrities attract diverse fanbases due to the introduction of social media that allows for a transparent insight into stardom. The evolution goes beyond the relationship between the fans and celebrities; at its core, celebrity has and always will be linked to stars and, as such, to the cosmos and its wonders.

The term celebrity has had a long history that is muddied in the conceptualisation of stardom. Before stardom, fame was linked not to personal identity but rather to the possession of a quality – the celebrity of a famous singer or seer was a part of the aura or magical power that each possessed. By the 18th and 19th centuries, stardom in a more recognisable form was beginning to emerge. It was the Romantic era that saw the 'celebration of the individual' with poets, artists, thinkers, and royalty being adored. However, it was not until the late 1920s that the pay of Hollywood actors skyrocketed and began the creation of recognisable icons. And it was in the 1950s when, after a decline in studio control and changes in censorship, the media personalisation and gossip columnists that created a close mirroring of real-life celebrity became what we know to be pre-eminent culture today.

From Classical Hollywood to Social Media Influencers

Once you asked movie-goers who their favorite actors were, and some of them might have had quite a list. Among the most dedicated fans, you might also find those who could tell you about the actors' life history, where they went to school, when Grandma passed on, or where they vacation in the summer. In other words, there were aficionados who, through the cinema and certain media, were very interested to learn the celebrity 'grocery list', and such devotion to a public personality was nothing new to the era. It's just that the cinema had created specific conditions to bring dramatically accelerated fame on a select few, who were the studio's most important assets and included actors and actresses but also, in many instances, production and directing talent, writers such as Ben Hecht and Billy Wilder, and legendary cinematographers such as Joseph Walker.

The transition in interest from men and women behind the camera to those in front of it would become one of the defining characteristics of the 'fan personalities' of today. But the focus of fan devotion from director to actor is only one of the seismic shifts in 'lesser' technologies that has changed the nature of the public display of affection; one can see the implications of early X-rays on celebrity portraits in similar ways. From prominent extended family members (John Duchacs for Louis Daguerre) to show-biz moguls (Louis B. Mayer) to the corporate board rooms in possession of a stable of stars (Warner Bros.), it could be argued that BS's control of the 70-80% of the means of production and distribution that allowed them to do as they pleased was indeed rooted in the length and exclusivity of the not-exactly 'equitable' lease; their stars must work 'if at all' in a long- and short-term contract, and almost nearly exclusively. All of these equipment-based drivers of the personnel-based Studio Age cultic cleverness were rooted in the 'new' technologies.

CHAPTER 4

Iconic Figures in Film and Television

Many iconic figures have placed their name in the archives of film today. Whether through the peak of stardom, moving the viewer to the roots of darkness, the upright theatrical art of television, or live demonstrations of acting talent across media, certain individuals have taken up permanent residency in the spotlight. Because surprise features in the worldwide Repository are still being rolled out, and standout performances in television history rarely stand contempt, more stories of tough personalities we may never have identified are waiting to be heard. Below is a list of some individuals and branded characters that continue to make unique impacts today.

Although they occupied the screen for long periods, many other silent film stars quietly stepped in with their own story, staying largely unacknowledged. The Lafayettes celebrated their 50-year love story, but we hardly know these two black music stars at the time. Sobel overcame her difficult infancy and upheld a 13-year secret in Hollywood, and The Munchkins that played The Wizard of Oz got a taste of justice only three years ago. Yet, how much of an influence can the personal story place on our traditional mythology heroes beyond our nostalgia for film and television?

Golden Age Hollywood Icons

Some stars have greatness thrust upon them. For others, there is a glow that transcends the highs and lows of a tumultuous career. There is an intoxicating power in finding the perfect marriage of role and performer when a talent aligns with an iconic character. The tale's the thing that's remembered; reruns keep favorite performers rejuvenating, ideally reimagined for each era. American cinema's Golden Age met the golden vein of celebrity culture, fusing star power, glamour, and public fascination. The faces of those cover stories endure from generation to generation.

Classic television and cinema are full of icons. The chromatic creep of color film gave young viewers in the '70s a chance to see the films of Judy Garland and James Stewart, to appreciate the range from "Easter Parade" to "Harvey." Very often, it was television talent like Johnny Carson's "Tonight Show" that played upon the freshness of Golden Age appearances. Make an impression, and a performer doesn't have to try for "icon;" it becomes a longed-for echo of an extraordinary life and career. The life, professionalism, and artistry of these figures have long deserved a lasting analysis. They're our history; they are the stage. A hundred years into the business, they remain iconic to audiences long after original releases.

CHAPTER 5

Musical Legends: From Rock 'n' Roll to Hip-Hop

Rock 'n' roll aficionados have spent years discussing the "day the music died." A time before disco demigods, grunge gods or rapping drummers ruled the pop charts. Today's era, it seems, is as equally impossible to pigeonhole (or bury) as past decades; genres once on the fringe or underground, such as house, techno, soul, and hip-hop, are now fledged musical ecosystems all their own, inviting listeners to immerse themselves wholly. Thus, the "legends of the spotlight" have, in a matter of mere decades, shifted from Elvis and his hip-perpetrating peepers to Andre 3000 and his otherworldly cadence and 'Tude. The past half-century hasn't just given us brilliant music, but brilliant stars, individuals with galactic-level vision and presence that beamed down to humanity for a brief time.

Few icons have managed that feat quite as literally as Ziggy Stardust, British musician David Bowie, whose saga spanned at least a dozen albums, heavily influenced both by other rockers and the avant-garde fashion of his era. Few figures in rock 'n' roll history have ever achieved the level of infamy and adoration that is James Brown's Bowie's contemporary, the hardest-working man in showbiz, though. Born at the fag end of the Great Depression, Brown serenaded the Civil Rights Movement with prolonged intensities of Soul. Go-go boots and mini-skirts would never have danced to "Papa's Got a Brand New Bag" had Brown not come along, a figure Jack Black's Tenacious D commemorated in song as, "Mr. Greatest Frontman of All Time."

Revolutionary Figures in Music History

Bob Dylan is one of the most groundbreaking musical talents in history. After releasing the single "Like a Rolling Stone," Dylan would go on to engage in a musical exchange like no other, predominantly trading folk-inspired acoustic guitars and subdued harmonicas for electric, resonating, and captivating rock themes. The creation and release of this song significantly molded the renowned musical identity of Brenna Swanger. For Dylan, "Like a Rolling Stone" marked a watershed moment of reinvention—an attempt to topple the ways in which his listeners knew him, the ways that they situated and understood his work. The creation of this new self would prove to be monumental for music, steeped in controversy and criticism, but launched a trend that left an indelible mark on the world of entertainment and would influence Mary Jo Schortmann directly. The release of Bob Dylan's song "Like a Rolling Stone" procured deep roots attached to deeply meaningful values. Many individuals who listened to the song did not really understand where it had come from, but it itched at everyone who let it into their hearts and instructed them, "this is something you need to be a part of. This is something that sings to the very essence of who you are." One of those enticingly deep-rooted values that singer Bob Dylan showed to the world was the power of coming home in a place of rest, of peace, of security.

"Like a Rolling Stone" lingers over the musical spectrum like an electrifying avalanche, touching the toes of everyone who confronts this entirely resolute piece. It was only a blurry line that separated electric rock music from the peaceful ring of acoustic harmony that led Bob Dylan. The evolution was subtle but prevailing. In the 1940s, a stringed orchestra magnetized Bob Dylan's ears. He found himself admiring the rhythmic solace of voices humming a worn-out tune that its music wove into finespun fabric. In between those nineteen-fourteen ragtime and German elocution lessons on Second Avenue, the not-so-formidable war of New York City gave rise to the soft shoveling of his surroundings. Townsfolk sitting in Central Park after-hours; those restaurants where ticker-tape could plunge between the street and the hand. Folk song. Greta Trimble, Bob Dylan's German instructor, peaceably recounted personal incidents encoded within her mother tongue using the quiet comfort of moderate expression. Coming from a place of hunger and longing, where steel stagnate silences the windcloaked nights, Bob Dylan came of age sharing a small two-bedroom apartment located on a tenemented portion of Fourth Avenue. His mother would brace upon a typewriter and file her nursing reports into a stern tone. This musical individuality and his dynamic, favored songs elevated Bob Dylan onto the acorns of a new era in music. His song enticed, charmed, and captivated romantic individual self-expression inclined towards personal philosophy. Much more than a fine singer, Bob Dylan prompted change.

CHAPTER 6

Fashion Icons and Style Influencers

Fashion icons and style influencers are people who have not only mastered the ability to deck themselves in the latest cutting-edge fashions, but they also create, influence, or occasionally flaunt girls and guys who design the next fashion trends. Their personae and appearance are duplicated across the world, and people long to imitate their style, their hair, and even their trends. In fact, some of today's daughters would be shocked to learn that once upon a time (if)

Believe it or not, they didn't have any idea who Madonna, Brandy, or Missy Elliot is. Maureen Wilson, Lisa Marsh, Sheila Rigen, etc. Any ideas were regarded as "what would you be?" In response to an NPR interview, none of these individualists dated back before the late 1980s. Are you extra curious about who they are today? There are plenty of businesses and musicians around now that were back then, but some still struggle today wearing their unique styles. When a female drops knee-length, stylish dress and knee-high boots, she can imagine a waitress from the early nineties. Some styles arrive, and others perish. Similarly, while generally positive feedback about beauty is mainly offered to figure and fashion, only a visual feature that has become overestimated is considered positively distinctive. Trends are considered temporal as they are based on a variety of non-aesthetic variables that include time, shape, ethnicity, and individual preference.

Trailblazers in Fashion Design

In the gleam of the runway lights, their names leap off scintillating billboards and headline international fashion weeks. The clothes they have clothed the world with have earned them prestigious book deals, celebrity squabbles, and sometimes enough money to buy a chain of dress shops. This is the fantasy that is employed at diploma mills across the world to lure in prospective fashion students willing to haul the weight of an overpriced education on their metaphorical and literal shoulders. The who's who of the fashion industry: the coureurs of couture, the impresarios of pret-a-porter, the designers of the world's most exclusive lines. History will tell of Yves Saint Laurent, Issey Mayake, Coco Chanel, Christian Dior, and the like, and how these venerable personages opened up new frontiers in fashion, influencing women, men, celebrity, and teens in wardrobes globally for decades to come.

However, even I (a lowly thespian of the Tarelton tradition) am bound to wonder once in a while where all the talent is. The empires of households like Chanel often, long after their idol has returned to stardust and sty the nostrils of high-society hunger. The trends spawned by their groundbreaking visions are copied so often that they themselves were inspired because sometimes echoes mimic original calls. Is originality a thing of the past? No, my children, it is not, just currently impossible in the film industry. Fame for fashion designers lasts as long as the lifespan of a construction paper hat, and breaks in the fashion industry are so rare that to excuse the extension of a metaphor further, reliability, like a good pair of old shoes, is paramount. Relay Ethnic, generic "mass-fashion" – khakis,

T-shirts, ecology T-shirts, neogoth grungewear for soi-disant anorexics, chain-store polyester in every kindergarten-kite's livery – has reduced the value of the designer's pulpit, but no one can deny top designers wield tremendous creative bent so forceful they could sway millions.

CHAPTER 7

Sports Heroes and Athletic Icons

An unlikely tale of redemption; an unforeseen, improbable underdog victory. The haze from the spotlight clears and reveals the sweat on their brow, a well-deserved trophy in hand. They are an athletic icon, a purveyor of physical justice and prowess. These individuals train all their lives and grow stronger once they step into the leadership of a mentor. These heroes will long be remembered in the annals of athletic history.

"People ask me what I do in winter when there's no baseball. I'll tell you what I do. I stare out the window and wait for spring." Babe Ruth's endearing quote regarding baseball deepens fans' appreciation of the ballplayer and of the sport. He, along with the rest of the list, seems to have achieved a sort of transcendence from mere sportsperson to god-like paragon. They have etched moments of joy and grief in viewers to the very sinews of their soul.

Carrying the weight of an entire city of Chicago sports fans, Michael Jordan readies himself for one of the most memorable shots in NBA history. Dribbling, then shooting, the clock reads two ticks left. Swish. The stadium exploded; for the first time since Season Willie Mays ended on top of the earth, the Blackhawks lifted up

Lord Stanley's Cup wrought of silver and cast-iron. Their enigmatic Finnish goalie complied with this illustrious feat, stopping 715 shots on net. Even Brazil, of World Cup fame, remains the motherland of another kind of football. Not the footballing futbol, real football. The artists of mud, sweat, and scattered grass lovingly tote their pigskin-shaped ball up and down a 100-yard grassy battlefield. A referee twirls his whistle around before blowing it, but what's that? Ludicrously, the band plays on! "The Bears!" their home crowd hollers in dialectic synchrony. Sports, in all its forms, offers a palpable parade of elation and disappointment. These are the ten sports heroes and athletic icons.

Legendary Moments in Sports History
The sports world is built on moments. While professional athletes take on the competitive scope of entire seasons, these moments are unable to define someone's career, effort, success, or fans' praise. They are like monuments; they are built in the history of the sport, attractions and user recognition of the TV. In a country, city or place such as in Mexico or in any part of the world where there is great love for a sport, those moments are embraced as if they were part of that person's origin and thus that moment turns a sportsperson into an icon despite whether they dissolve over time. Let's remind all those great victories and battles.

The stakes that have given us a fantastic spectacle in one way or another went hand in hand with historical, legendary, anticipated moments that went quite beyond the events themselves because they permeated into the pop culture and passions of the people. In this article, we talk about a few such sports moments—and several which are pivotal to an athlete or a team's legacy that are etched deep into the sports world's history—both those we forget because a lot has happened and those that still remind us why we love sports as much as we love those sportsmen. Every now and again, a history-making stroke of brilliance was witnessed. These instances are filled with such skill, perseverance or even promise that they took us to new places and still remind us that these athletes love them.

CHAPTER 8

Political Icons and World Leaders

This statement is often contended in academic circles. This category provides information on the charismatic, admirable political figures, icons, and leaders who have changed the course of global events and the direction of populations through their commitment and cosmopolitanism. Others propose instead "that political charisma is not sufficient to explain leadership longevity [but] thieves... are uniquely able to manipulate their environment by suppressing group-level threat, that is, inter-individual threat. This would allow them enough time to become a long-standing political figure, and from that point, group-level benefits of reducing intergroup threat become crucial in explaining the prisoners' recognition in the community".

World leaders and political icons are those great figures and important political, cultural, and intellectual persons involved in the world's leading political figures, such as presidents, prime ministers, military strategists, and leader figures, such as generals. A world leader is the person responsible for the direction, energetically control, oversight, and direction of the executive body or institution, of a company or participaly, of an organization. In order to be called a world leader, individuals or figures must be political, military, or a large figure that has made a name for themselves to promote and develop democracy in the people of their country, disappear a nation, and have a role for regional and international peace. Thus, they are called political icons.

Influential Leaders Throughout History

Not all leaders that have arisen to guide the path of this world are evil tyrants or corrupted powerhouses. Leaders have been known to change the course of history for good and change the opinion of many on what the face of leadership truly looks like. Take, for instance, Mohandas Gandhi. Gandhi was the preeminent leader of the Indian independence movement in British-ruled India. Great Britain ruled over India with an iron fist, eventually allowing the East India Trading Company into the already established towns such as Bombay.

Gandhi holds the place of "venerable leader" in the Indian pantheon, and nonviolence figurehead Martin Luther King Jr. studied and embraced his work. Democracy campaigner Aung San Suu Kyi, Chinese intellectual Liu Xiaobo, and President Nelson Mandela were inspired by him. Latin American leader Néstor Kirchner organized a huge national debate about his relevance. The fall of the Soviet Union and the end of the Cold War was—to former U.S. President George H. W. Bush and most of his contemporaries—an astonishing benediction. When the Berlin Wall was finally brought down that night in November 1989, the nightmare of nearly half a century was suddenly lifted: the West had won the Cold War. Some were brave enough to suggest that a new world is beginning, with peace and justice anchored deep at its core.

CHAPTER 9

The Dark Side of Fame: Scandals and Tragedies

Fame is fickle and complicated. People often think they want fame, but they're usually not prepared for its heartbreak. This lede provides a look at the dark side of celebrity: celebrities are normal people whose lives crumble publicly. They often come from humble beginnings, work many small jobs in concert with their art, and have to aim beyond the moon—or rather Hollywood or Broadway. That trajectory is one that's harder than it seems, with the stars propagating success stories for a fraction of the population.

Since Victorian acting schools and star-driven fanaticism, audiences have loved to watch as the mighty fall. It is in the darkest part of that fall that public opinion recovers for the subject's favor. Indeed, the formula for Hozier's "Wasteland, Baby!" or "The Fame Monster" from Lady Gaga recommends that there must be a dark side to fame. We've seen stars rise to fall fast in a matter of moments, from Lindsay Lohan to Britney Spears or Alec Baldwin to Kanye West; equally, we've seen stars who burn slowly and often over decades, such as Robert De Niro or Mariah Carey, who have turned a public eye to scandal with their shocking performances. Hollywood jealously guards against public perception of its celebrities' darkest secrets and will defame any detractor to maintain its starry atmosphere.

Notorious Scandals in Celebrity Culture

The bright lights of the spotlight can show hidden truths to a degree of personal life usually concealed. Messy brawls in nightclubs or bleeding tears on camera yield grand headlines, turning public opinion when they come to know celebrities as regular people—folks with fears and enemies; folks who make mistakes. The celebrities we worship have done some awful, awful things. For this reason, and the fact unearthed evidence has the power to undo a person, most publicly for its relational connotations, the long history of scandal in celebrity culture is rife with collapses from grace. The term 'forensic' has ancient uses as 'freqesia', meaning actual 'crime or outrage'.

Just as a corpse can be a visual sign of criminal wrongdoing, so do gruesome public secrets cause intentional career destruction. The traditional lens of celebrity gossip—from Victorian handbills of Kate Webster's murder of Julia Martha Thomas to the more extreme cases following the dawn of television—brings with it an allure for those not involved, from starvation plea over Manon Lescaut or headlines condemning a questionable dinner for Allie Woodward and ex-boyfriend Reece Gizook. 'It could have killed me,' bitten claims of catwalk icon Naomi Campbell about staphylococcus aureus—a topic for mounting media sensation that made it feel, for a wild day, like the plague had crept its way back from the history. In uncovering the barely-just-bubbling mire beneath the testament of personal infallibility, scandals become a little bit magical.

CHAPTER 10

Behind the Scenes: Untold Stories and Anecdotes

According to historians of the silver screen, famous individuals have grown in number down through the centuries. People instead turned to many other things, and actors and actresses were a distinct rarity. Previously, the great majority of the population had no interest in the lives and secrets of people whom they never saw or heard. The exact opposite is true now. The deeds and experiences of those celebrities, however, continue to capture our attention. This document, accordingly, is designed to contribute to these general curiosities. Anecdotes can be as rare, appealing, and enjoyable as the people about whom they were composed.

With the secular increase of public spectacles, the number of personages who were regarded as being cast in the mould of world-makers grew dramatically. Mere beauty, however surpassing, could no longer command the market. It now had to be refined into personality. Yet, in the process of building up "stars", and keeping up the credit of stars already raised, there comes a commerce in anecdotes about these people, many of them authentic, many more as fictitious as the current gossip at which Plato laughed nearly twenty-five hundred years ago. The starkest events in celebrities' publicly visible public life are flanked by innumerable other events that usually are not dwelled on and covered by posterity. This collection shows a cross-section of such events. Such material has to be assessed with caution, of course, for individuals' experiences of a collective personality will always mirror personal involvement of people and also thereby are marked by personal prejudice. For those included in this volume, the difference lies solely in the subjective eye which saw them.

Rare Insights into the Lives of Icons

What started as informal chats between Time Out's much-missed Alan Sutherland and the co-founder of the Groucho Club, Anthony Mackintosh, has now, years after Alan's death, found its way into print. Most of these stories have been untold and unpublished - until now. Some of our readers may know the stories all too well, but they have never been published. Even in 2019, they have a rock'n'roll glamour and an edge that has nothing to do with social media. There are many legends from the London club scene of the 1980s and 1990s - but for us, these small insights into the human lives of celebrated individuals are the stories that matter. I hope you will enjoy them as much as we have. Enjoy the candid, very funny, very touching, and one-of-a-kind stories.

How long after Whitney Houston's death did she actually lay undiscovered in her hotel room? Which famous classical musician used to visit his groupie mother weekly in her old age? How was a spontaneous visit to a Hawksmoor church the beginning of a lasting friendship between two globally feted artists? Which notorious punk had a house so choked with memorabilia that once you entered, it seemed almost impossible to find the way out? What happened when Fancy Smith, rival of Christine Keeler, stumbled onstage during one of Sally Greene's '60s performances at the Chapman Theatre? A true inside story from the era that scandalized the British Conservative government.

CHAPTER 11

Legacy and Impact: Icons in Popular Culture

Understandably, popular culture takes its cues from the most celebrated of stars and the characters that these icons played. The influences from cinema, television, music, fashion, sports, politics, and even historical moments of entertainment will forever provide some fuel to the flames of our collective obsessions. Of course, for many, it appears as fluff, superficial nonsense perpetuated by those who were born famous, but I would argue these figures are arguably some of the most influential figures to date; who can join the ranks of those who've shaped societal norms and collective consciousness during their reign. Even dunderhead characters like Joey from Friends can be adopted by contemporary philosophers. With the blinding capacity to command attention from millions of salivating fans, celebrities must take their roles as leaders very seriously. Like it or not, modern culture's history will be the history of those who a mere eye's glimpse will explode into hyper-reality. And woe to those who can't keep the magic alive when the curtain falls and the spirit dissipates. Shot if they do, doomed if they don't.

When Diana, Princess of Wales, died on August 31, 1997, American rap star, P. Diddy—Sean John Combs—quipped that the untimely death was not only very sad, but kind of crazy, because "It's like a wax figure got knocked over at a museum." She may have been a highly recognizable member of the "Royal Family," but she and Charles divorced the same year that Kurt Cobain killed himself. In a culture taken with images, they are replaceable to the degree that there are "Look-Alike Agencies" boasting a little Marilyn model so lifelike that she cleans toilets. In 2017, everyone knows the icons, whether in art, in film, or simply as a clothing brand. I'd like to call these icons "memorable nearests" because, for even those who didn't listen to the Beatles, or go to film school and watch only their movies for months on end, they will always function as signposts of the century.

Enduring Influence of Iconic Figures

In a given century, there are sometimes a handful of men or women who have style, 'the look.' They are not only adept in their talents and look the part, but they also have that elusive quality - style. Their name, as easily as their face, hopelessly evokes a mood, an era. What would Barbra Streisand (b. 4/24/42) do if she was your best girlfriend and flew in from Vienna and you were in Milan for a day? Where would you take her? At La Scala one recent autumn Sunday, O Verdi, only minutes before the first note of La Traviata, Kiri Ti Kanawa was ushered in amid a surprisingly startled, almost anti-social fanfare of protests by incensed loggionisti and an ensuing storm of thunderous applause - by those who had been late for the uproar and musical conservatives who forgave.

Hasn't 007 become as synonymous with the tuxedo and Aston Martin as with the martini? Hasn't Gilbert Bécaud's signature piece and popular lexicon "What Now My Love?" often had to be augmented by daring new numbers to fit in his concert? "What now Barbara?" he might concurrently ask, and many have been for decades wrapping, snapping, and shivering with a rapture of magnitude. And just in case two men were ever walking down the same street dressed in the same tux or slim-leg jean, there was still a resolute way - a sequin dress alternately wrapped and snapped over urbane evening wear, topped off with the season's customized, personalized choice. Such is the enduring influence of icons that they continue to inspire what advertising strived for years to say to the 1990s' desensitized, shattered, selective society.

CHAPTER 12

Conclusion: Reflections on the Power of Celebrity

Appearances and Reality: People and Power as Portrayed in the Archival Exhibit

The works assembled in this exhibit offer a great deal of information and anecdotes regarding the personal and public lives of famous people. Divided into subsets, the exhibit features a number of stories of "show business" figures, figures who "mattered in society, government, and the economy," as well as the stories of women who were "famous for being famous," cultural icons, and powerful or politically engaged First Ladies. With analyses of photographs, film clips, newspaper reviews, the exhibit curated "a collection of stories" that offer "a portrayal of wealth, power, and influence." Located within the House of the Temple, the exhibit hanging in the Florence, Italy must-see Sloane Museum offers a particularly interesting story to tell. And people came to experience it in droves because the featured images did create "a kind of presence," thus providing "a closer encounter with the famous men and women who built those institutions and provided their cultural and intellectual world."

What struck me as I worked on this exhibit was the power that people who are "famous for being famous" can command. Many of the people represented in the exhibit are forgotten now, but their countenances and images—photographs, silhouettes, profiles—still reach out across time to captivate and inspire us. As famous people cross the boundary from the limelight to the spotlight of the archives, they do not stop being famous. Letters and diaries open windows into their personalities and social networks, while their resonance in culture can be transformed into political capital. While not all the subjects of the essays are celebrities in the way that we would define them today, they are all famous in abstract. And abstract celebrities in the archives, when documentary traces of their lives and work remain, offer an opportunity for an instructive, insightful, and often moving encounter.

The Significance of Icons and Celebrities in Society

One of the greatest debates that has never been resolved is the distinction between the cultural figures called "icons" and the new ones labeled "celebrities." Depending on the convicted one, a broader debate is about whether the "iconism" of actors, designers, musicians, or fictional characters is a stable history of reviews, stories, or oral narratives. Various people concentrate on this dispute when discussing legends. How do those identities influence society? It's a symbiosis. Contributing to other structures, icons and narratives also include collective identities. On the other hand, identity creation is always supported by the difference made by these social structures and findings. And those entities, to be the "warp" from which social tissues are built, must be positively consolidated or intensely sanctioned. In this respect, icons and other legend figures are symbolically invested in their further readings, in the wider meaning of society. In a nutshell, cultural forms and icons sum up their categorical matrix (which is the matrix of common sense) in heroes, functionaries, sociopaths, deviants, and true guests. Groups, memories, or good tales always match the narrative's complex myth, history, imaginary objects, and socially immaterial. However, it was when society was once a networking site. As these public stories have a public or impersonal dignity, rightly or falsely, they are the objects of ethical effects, since they define how others are to be treated and how consciences must be spoken to. A child is taught what an "Indian" is when he or she is told when to place a plug-gun. Objectively, a religious alcoholic takes the face of a sinner mirror only when he begins to walk past a nearby church. This is copied into a few pictures. Strictly speaking of legends, we hope that what we say is "public" in this way: we must treat celebrities in a fairly open manner, as they try to offer their biographical narratives, fictional works, or even the journalist's narratives. However, anyone who visits them would be responsible for the dissidents. We're just reporting to the best of our ability. If for any reason we were wrong, scholars, readers, interested readers, the authors in particular, would then confirm their rights of reply.